OVERVIEW

As more and more organizations globally have mobile employees on international assignment and extended business trips, it is crucial to think proactively how to manage and mitigate tax risks associated with the expatriates. New, aspiring, and even experienced professionals often look for guidance when in difficult situations.

Managing tax risks associated with the expatriates can be a challenge for Global Mobility, Immigration, Human Resources, Finance and Tax professionals as they are not experts. Unfortunately, the market does not cater to any easy-to-read guide on global mobility tax issues that will help understand such risks.

"Essentials of Global Mobility Tax" hand book is an attempt to bridge this gap to empower tax and non-tax professionals understand such complex topics in a simplified manner that makes the topics more interesting!

This book culminates my personal experience and learning in expatriate and mobility tax management of over fifteen years. These learning's are categorized into separate chapters related to each phase of international assignment. The book will help readers understand mobility tax from a global perspective and take essential steps in supervising and handling the program proficiently.

 # TABLE OF CONTENTS

CHAPTER 1

EXPATRIATE TAX

GUIDE

Organizations that have employees travelling on business trip or short term/long term assignments overseas must ensure they put in place a robust system that oversees the complete assignment life cycle starting from Immigration to Tax compliance in home/host country during and end of assignment.

Having a good Tax Equalization program ensures the organization is serious about the program and most importantly working diligently for its globally mobile employees comply with worldwide employee tax obligations. These obligations arise when employees become subject to foreign income or social tax as a result of an international assignment or international business travel.

An international assignment is generally defined as company-sponsored travel from one country to another country for a temporary period of time ranging from 31 days to 3 years.

Employees on approved international assignments or business trips should be covered under Tax Equalization Policy. The intent of tax equalization is to ensure the employee pays a similar amount of income/social tax that he/she would have paid if they had not worked overseas. These payroll filings require organizations to report taxable wages and deposit income or social tax on behalf of employees covered by the Tax Equalization program. Under tax equalization, companies will be responsible for paying income or social tax as a result of these calculations.

If a company is starting to send employees abroad, it needs to assess its administrative capabilities. Can they handle complicated tasks, such as systems set-up, split payrolls and tax burden? Often, international assignment leads to outsourcing for global expertise. Immigration, Tax, Payroll, Employment Law requires an investment in sound professional advice.

Due to lack of global expertise and complexities most organizations engage professional tax services provider to assist with the administration of tax equalization process. The tax services provider assists from Immigration (securing work visa) to various host country compliance activities such as Income and Social Tax ID registrations for employees, Employer registrations, Shadow payroll calculations, Income and Social tax payment guidance/assistance, Employer/Employee tax returns filings, coordination with local authorities and handling responses to Employer/Employee notices during/post repatriation.

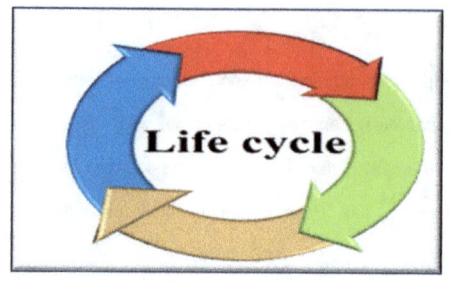

CHAPTER 2

ASSIGNMENT

LIFE

CYCLE

Companies tend to spend a significant amount of time, financial and human resources planning and coordinating on international assignments. Cost of international assignments is one of the top mobility-related concerns of global employers. The international assignment process is commonly considered to encompass **four distinct phases**: pre-assignment stage, assignment initiation stage, actual assignment stage and post-assignment stage referred to as repatriation.

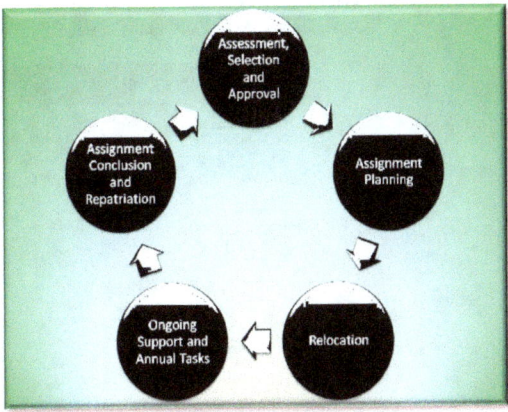

Below is a simple process follow that will help understand the activities and roles by concerned teams within and outside the organization to ensure smooth international assignment.

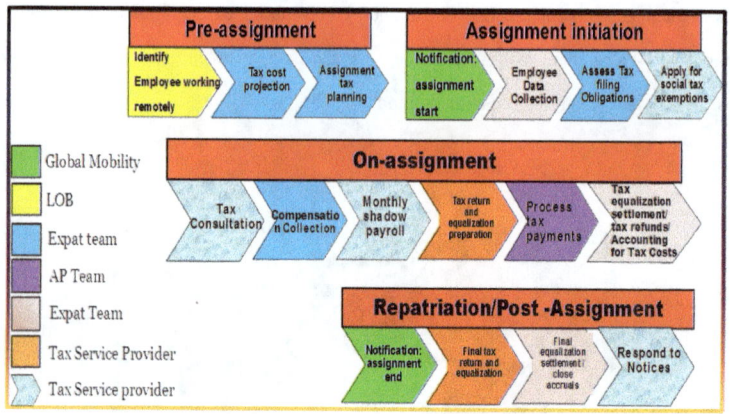

CHAPTER 3

PRE-

ASSIGNMENT

(TO DO)

Tax Cost projection:

Every organization must build a cost estimator tool to assist bid /project managers in estimating Mobility Costs (mainly immigration costs, tax costs and travel expenses,) that should be incorporated into the Bid Profitability Workbook if non-local staffing/foreign consultants are planned or will be used to deliver services in the host country/project country.

The following categories should get covered in the cost estimator:

- Visa/Work permit costs and acquisition fees

- Travel Expenses, including Airfare, Accommodation (Hotel/Rental) and Meals/Incidental costs

- Minimum Wage Requirement (MWR) - A minimum salary or prevailing wage required to be paid to the consultant under local country laws

- Employee taxes that will be charged to the project owning cost centre, such as Income Taxes, Social taxes, Social Insurance, other payroll related taxes and associated tax preparation fees

Cost estimator tool should compute tax and social security using:

- Average base salary (midpoint) for each home country, based on the resource level selected

- Estimated annual/quarterly bonus payable at 100% of target

- Travel expenses, to the extent such items are taxable under local law

- Minimum Salary or Prevailing wage, if applicable

- Exclusion of Personal income/deductions

- Compute home and host country income and social tax costs in accordance with local country laws

- Exclude host country tax if the onsite days are less than De Minimis day's threshold

Stake holder's consensus

It is quite important to involve key stake holders such as Global Mobility, Immigration, Employment Legal, Finance, Expat Tax and Business during the bid stage as having consensus and approvals from all stake holders is critical to ensure project can be managed and complied as per host country laws. If any stake holder has reservations on the host compliance necessary risk factors should be weighed to analyse the quantum before proceeding.

CHAPTER 4

IMMIGRATION

RESPONSIBILITIES

Immigration plays a key role in ensuring the expatriates are applying and working in the host country on correct visa that allows them to legally stay and work on client projects that will not have any adverse impact on the client and company reputation. Immigration must track the visa validity period to ensure expatriates do not overstay without valid permit. Extension applications must be initiated well in advance if project requires stay beyond the visa validity period.

Once an individual is chosen for an assignment, Immigration must move quickly to secure the necessary visas. Requirements and processing times vary by country. Immigration should start by contacting the host country's consulate or embassy for information on visa requirements. Visa norms being complex in nature many organizations seek external Immigration services provider assistance to ensure smooth management of the visa application/renewal process. In many countries in the event immigration authorities ascertain expatriates are working in country with incorrect work visa both client and organization sending expatriate can be blacklisted for non-compliance.

Following is a list of generic visa types that may be required depending on the nature of business to be conducted in a particular country:

- A work permit authorizes paid employment in a country

- A work visa authorizes entry into a country to take up paid employment

- A dependent visa permits family members to accompany or join employees in the country of assignment

- A multiple-entry visa permits multiple entries into a country

CHAPTER 5

GLOBAL

MOBILITY

RESPONSIBILITIES

Preparing for the Assignment:

An international assignment agreement that outlines the specifics of the assignment and documents agreement by the employer and the expatriate is necessary. Global Mobility is responsible for issuance of appropriate letter of assignment (LOA) or agreement.

In practice assignment letters, or assignment agreements, often consist of little more than confirmation of the assignment location and job title, without giving details of assignment duration, compensation, tax, benefits and other important issues. The lack of such information leaves much to interpretation and may cause considerable disruption at a later stage if employees have a different understanding of how a particular issue, for example tax on personal income, will be treated while on assignment.

By setting up a comprehensive assignment letter which is discussed in detail with and then signed by the employee prior to the assignment, such conflicts can be avoided. Expectations are managed at the outset and assignment terms and conditions are clear to all involved, particularly the employee, but also home and host Mobility and line managers.

Furthermore, the document will serve as clarification for other departments such as Payroll or Finance as well as for external parties, in particular, the company's tax service providers. In the event of an audit by the tax authorities, it is very common for tax authorities to request copies of relevant assignment letters. It is therefore crucial that the assignment agreement correctly reflects the assignment terms and is in line with how the assignment is actually managed in practice, in particular with regard to assignment compensation and the corresponding treatment of tax and social security.

So, how detailed should an assignment agreement be? The answer is as detailed as possible. The assignment letter should be a legally binding document, confirming the agreement between the company and the employee with respect to the terms and conditions of the assignment. In reality, the most common approach is that the employee remains employed with the home company and the home employment contract remains in place.

However, the assignment letter serves as an addendum to the employment contract and confirms the terms and conditions which vary from the normal contract while on assignment. Any terms and conditions not specifically varied therefore remain as per the home employment contract.

Most of the checklist items will require considerable scoping – particularly if no assignment policy exists, but making well outlined provisions will prove worthwhile. The extent to which each item should be explained is illustrated below for three key areas.

Compensation and Tax arrangements

This is possibly the most complex and important part of the assignment letter and must clearly explain how the employee will be compensated while on assignment. If the company uses a build-up or balance sheet approach, this section of the agreement should confirm details such as the home notional salary, cost of living adjustments, assignment and location allowances and assignment salary.

It should be confirmed whether the assignment salary is guaranteed net or gross, as well as where and how it will be delivered, i.e., through which payroll, currency, details of split pay arrangements, exchange rates, etc. If the company has a variable pay structure details of how bonus and incentive payments will be calculated and delivered while on assignment must also be included.

Employees will normally remain in home country social security plans while on assignment, subject to the relevant regulations, and this should also be confirmed in the assignment letter. This section of the agreement should also capture details of the tax services provided to the employee, e.g., departure and arrival briefings, tax return preparation, tax and social security registration, etc.

Assignment benefits

The most significant benefits, both in terms of cost to the company as well as value to the employee, are education allowances for the employee's children and host country accommodation. The assignment letter should clearly explain the level of benefits provided and how they are delivered, i.e. in-kind or in cash, bearing in mind the most tax effective form of delivery for the company depending on host country tax legislation. Tax charged on assignment benefits can be considerable, sometimes up to 50% of total assignment costs.

With education benefits it is important to state the type of schooling for which the company will provide assistance. If there are limits on the amount up to which the company will pay for education, or limitations on the choice of schools, this should be confirmed.

Similarly, the limits up to which the company will pay for host country accommodation must be set out clearly. The letter should also clarify what happens if the employee chooses accommodation below or above the set rental limits.

End of assignment

If there is the possibility of an assignment extension beyond the initially-agreed term, the applicable policy should be detailed here. Most importantly, a maximum duration beyond which the assignment will not be extended should be indicated.

It is also good practice to give details of the company's localisation policy in this section. It may well suffice to confirm that a localisation policy may be applied once the maximum assignment duration has been reached, without having to give too many details on the actual process.

The assignment letter is a crucial document which, if set up properly and in detail, will potentially help avoid much conflict and ensure the smooth administration of the assignment. However, an incomplete or inconsistent agreement can cause considerable disruption to the company and the employee. A company should always seek legal advice should a labour dispute arise.

Assignment letter checklist

The assignment letter should detail:

- ❖ The assignment starting date and planned duration
- ❖ The job title for the assignment role and the reporting line
- ❖ The location of the assignment and the work itself
- ❖ Whether the assignment is accompanied or unaccompanied by family members
- ❖ Contractual arrangements - including details of the employing and assignment companies' working hours
- ❖ Pre-assignment arrangements – provision and requirements for work permits, relocation benefits, cultural/language training
- ❖ Tax, social security and pension arrangements
- ❖ Details of the compensation, including the basis for salary reviews, bonuses, etc.
- ❖ Assignment benefits – including host country housing, education, holiday entitlement, home leave, air fare from assignment location for self and family members, medical insurance, utilities, telephone, transportation at host location, etc.
- ❖ Code of Ethics and Business Conduct
- ❖ Financial Assistance Program (country specific)
- ❖ Assignment end – conditions for possible assignment extension, repatriation, localisation, termination and resignation

Tracking assignment details

International assignment management is one of the hardest areas for Mobility/Human Resource professionals to master—and one of the costliest. The expense of a three-year international assignment can cost millions, yet many organizations fail to get it right. Despite their significant investments in international assignments, companies still report a high percentage of failure rates in these assignments.

With so much at risk, global organizations must invest in automation that will make international assignments successful. Knowing what to expect from start to finish as well as having the right details captured in the tool can help minimize the risk.

The mobility tool should generate periodic reports that identify the expected assignment end date at least a couple of months before completion and have a systemic trigger to the Project Manager to confirm status on extension or likely completion of the international assignment.

The international assignment automation tool should capture:

- ❖ Employee name and email id
- ❖ Type of assignment
- ❖ Assignment expected start date
- ❖ Assignment actual start date
- ❖ Assignment expected end date
- ❖ Assignment actual end date
- ❖ Home and Host location
- ❖ Host work country/state/city
- ❖ Type of visa and validity period
- ❖ Visa sponsor details – Client, Third Party, Host company
- ❖ Dependant details accompanying (if any)
- ❖ Project & Client details
- ❖ Host Project Manager name and email id

CHAPTER 6

EXPATRIATE

TAX

RESPONSIBILITIES

Expatriate tax matters have become increasingly complex, with home and host locations expanding into developing countries. Tax professionals face a difficult task. The role of expatriate tax ("employer") revolves around the following actions when it comes to tax:

- Determine overall policy strategy and treatment (tax equalization, tax protection)

- Establish hypothetical tax formulas and ensure appropriate tax withholdings

- Manage the services of the external tax provider

- Ensure compliance with home and host tax regulations

Key Focus Areas:

- ❖ Cost Projection

- ❖ Tax Policy & Treatment

- ❖ Tax Equalisation Programs

- ❖ Assignment Structuring

- ❖ Hypothetical (Hypo) Tax

- ❖ Business Travellers - challenges posed

- ❖ Travel Calendar – employee tracking

- ❖ Ensure Compliance with Local Tax Regulations

- ❖ Global Compensation – collection, review, distribution

- ❖ Shadow Payroll

- ❖ Tax Equalisation Settlements (TEQ)

- ❖ Manage services of Tax Services Provider

The following discussion provides an overview of each aspect and issues to be considered by Expatriate tax when making policy decisions.

Cost Projection

The decision to send an employee on an international assignment in a cost-conscious environment comes with multiple challenges. It is advantageous for Expatriate tax to determine any cost-saving opportunities where tax obligations – home, host, or both – can be lowered. For example, since fiscal years vary by country, a company can schedule an assignment and/or alter the timing of bonuses or allowances to take advantage of tax savings.

It is crucial to ensure compliance with residency rules that determine whether an expatriate is responsible for taxes to the home, host, or both countries. Time spent going over cost estimates can strengthen the understanding and trust between Expatriate tax and decision makers. Implementing a process of cost estimates before contracts are signed can assist Expatriate tax in gaining a reputation for being a true strategic partner in managing and steering the international assignment program toward success as finally everything boils down to "**the bottom line**".

Tax Policy and Treatment

International assignments are complicated by tax regulations both at home and host country. Home country and foreign tax laws, as well as a company's policy, should determine how the employer will treat the employee's income from investments and other sources not related to the company, any property ownership, and other such matters.

In general, majority of companies attempt to focus their programs, including the treatment of income tax, around the following principles:

- The employee will neither gain nor suffer undue financial burden as a result of the special circumstances and complexity of compensation and tax matters while on an international assignment

- The employee and employer must comply fully with the tax laws and filing requirements of both home and host governments

- Tax policies are fair and reasonable, to all employees, cost-effective, easy to administer, and easy to understand

From host country perspective, most governments require that an expatriate pays taxes on income attributed to working in that country, irrespective of where the income is actually paid. Expatriates' home country tax obligations may vary.

Although most countries do not require non-residents to report (or be taxed on) income earned outside the country, many expatriates still have continuing home country tax obligations from non-employment income, such as investments. Tax liability is likely to be higher on assignment due to higher foreign tax rates and payment of additional expatriate allowances.

In many countries, expatriate taxes are higher when compared to the home country tax system because the individual does not have the same opportunities to reduce local tax liability as do local employees. While certain concessions may be available for expatriates, such as advantageous tax rates and deductions or credits, individual circumstances may not always allow employees to claim deductions as their local counterparts. There can always be situations where the host country taxes are lower, resulting in a boon that would benefit either to the employee or company, depending on how the company handles taxes.

Many companies provide a number of diverse allowances on a tax-free basis to help employees pay for additional expenses related to the assignment – relocation, housing, car, hardship, children's schooling, and so on. Although these allowances are often paid on a tax-free basis, they are considered by many countries as taxable income, thereby raising overall income and resulting in a higher tax liability.

There are generally four common methods of treating expatriate tax:

- Tax Equalization
- Tax Protection
- Ad-hoc Treatment
- Laissez Faire

+ **"Tax Equalization"** — is consistent with the balance sheet approach to international compensation; the expatriate is no better or worse off financially as a result of the assignment

+ **"Tax Protection"** — the employer is responsible for the employee's tax liability if income taxes are higher than what the employee would have paid at home. The individual keeps any windfall when taxes are lower, but this result may raise an issue of inequity with colleagues in other locations. As a result, the employee might suffer a negative cash flow until the company reimburses the amount owed

+ **"Ad-Hoc"** — means that there is no formal tax policy, and the company handles each expatriate's tax situation on a case-by-case basis. The possibility exists for inequitable and inconsistent treatment of expatriate tax

+ **"Laissez Faire"** — places the entire responsibility on the employee for calculating and paying income taxes related to both home and host countries. Among possible results are potential calculation errors wherein host taxes are either lower or higher, and could result in noncompliance with government requirements

– The latter two are rarely used considering risks involved.

Tax Equalisation Programs:

Advantages

- Companies that send employees overseas typically assist them with the added costs they may incur (housing, cost-of-living, school tuition). Such benefit payments are generally taxable income to the employee and can increase his or her individual tax burden

- A tax equalisation program is a voluntary system by which both the employer and the employee pay their respective shares of the latter's global tax burden. The program, in essence, provides that the employee will pay neither more nor less tax while on assignment than if he or she had remained at home country payroll

- A tax equalisation program provides a company with several advantages.

  - **Simplicity** – The employee generally will not suffer a tax "penalty" as a result of the international assignment

  - **Fairness** – Employees sent to different tax jurisdictions will be treated equally (in terms of taxes)

Disadvantages

- Cost to the employer can go up, especially if the employee is sent to a country with a much higher tax rate

- Cost exposure for the employer may increase if the employee incurs a high level of "personal" taxable income (for example, from stock options) while on the assignment. (Capping the amount of "personal" income the program covers can mitigate the cost)

Assignment Structuring/Tax Planning

There are many ways of structuring an international assignment. Many companies develop a special policy in which the structures of international assignments are described, and the applicable labour conditions are defined.

- **"Secondment"** – In this situation, the employment agreement in the home country remains in place. The employee will however, be seconded temporarily to an employer in the host country. Usually, this is a company that belongs to the same group of companies the home company belongs

- **"Split employer"** – In this situation, the employee will work at home as well as the home country for two different formal employers. The employer-employee relationship is defined in two various employment agreements. This setup is also known as the "split salary"

Hypothetical (Hypo) Tax

Hypothetical tax, is subtracted from base salary and retained by the employer, approximates the amount that would be paid by home-country at a comparable salary level. For practical purposes, making a hypothetical deduction is easier than calculating the employee's actual tax liability, which requires details of various financial circumstances.

The employer uses hypothetical tax to pay home and host country taxes. If foreign authorities prohibit an employer from paying employees' foreign taxes directly, employees are then responsible for payment (with reimbursement by the employer). The expatriate may also be responsible for home country tax payments on non-company source income (such as investments).

The employer withholds a hypothetical income tax assessed against compensation at the same level as that assessed for home-country. In turn, the employer is responsible for tax assessed on company-earned income (e.g., base salary, bonus). If taxes are higher on assignment, the employer reimburses the difference; if they are lower, the company retains the savings.

Business Travellers – challenges posed

The compliance environment is changing, bringing more focus on capturing correct income and collecting tax on business travellers. In most countries Immigration and Tax authorities have been partnering with each other. The 183-day rule applies only between countries with treaties under certain conditions and often does not apply at all if the employee's expenses are being charged to the foreign company.

The types of services that the employee is performing in the foreign country also need to be carefully reviewed, as they may be regarded by local tax authorities as directly benefiting the local company and, therefore, immediately taxable.

Expatriate Tax should consider the option of establishing processes to identify business travellers and capture/report data. In general, extended travellers (short-term) fall under equalisation policies/processes, but frequent business travellers are not supported under tax equalisation.

Expatriate Tax should also consider taking action to ensure tax and visa compliance of extended business travellers and short-term assignments. Many companies thus rely on external tax and immigration service providers to monitor and advise them on potential compliance issues.

Travel Calendar – Employee Tracking

Companies should implement a system requiring all employees on international assignment or business travel covered under tax equalisation program to report home and host country travel days in the form of Travel Calendar.

Travel Calendar should capture all work and non-work days inclusive of any business or vacation trip outside of host location. The Travel Calendar should be updated for the entire Tax year period of home and host country.

Additionally gathering data from external provider (e.g., company travel agent) to track and report employee travel is also beneficial as this can help reconcile miss-outs/gaps.

Ensure Compliance with Local Tax Regulations

Companies sending employees abroad, through international assignment or frequent business travellers, will probably incur additional tax liability on employees' global compensation. Being ill-prepared or ignoring various countries reporting requirements can be very costly for the company in terms of fines, fees, and administration costs.

Many countries can and will impose criminal penalties on company representatives for misreporting employee compensation, whether or not the employees are country residents.

It is critical that both the organization and the employees who fall into these categories understand the level of risk associated with working in a global environment. The fact that every country has its own set of compliance requirements some of which can be quite stringent complicates the level of risk.

An employee's income may be subject to tax in both home and host locations regardless of where earned, paid, or received. This income includes assignment allowances and expenses for items such as cost-of-living, housing, foreign tax, education, gross ups, hypothetical withholding, and relocation.

Similarly, equity plans may be subject to host country taxes even if paid after the employee returns home. These factors would thus require companies to capture all income and report in both home and host locations to avoid problems with tax regulators.

Global Compensation – collection, review, distribution

Many countries require Income and Social Security taxes to be paid on a monthly/quarterly basis.

Companies thus engage external tax services provider to assist with the administration of the tax equalization process. The tax services provider need to arrange monthly payroll filings with local tax authorities for Income Tax and Social Security. These payroll filings require companies to report taxable wages and deposit income or social tax on behalf of employees covered by the Tax Equalization program.

Under tax equalization, employers are responsible for paying income and/or social tax as a result of these calculations. Apart from monthly shadow payroll, tax services provider needs to prepare employee tax filings, such as individual income tax returns (monthly/quarterly/half yearly/year-end) as per local regulations.

Collection:

Tax services providers for tax calculations generally require details such as monthly/annual pay stubs, expense reimbursement in host country, stock options vested/exercised, insurance premium paid by employer and any employer benefit provided to employee during assignment as these could be taxable in hands of employee in host country.

In order to get this organised Expatriate Tax needs to coordinate with various teams within home country to gather compensation data. Expatriate tax needs to collate and share the compensation data within stipulated timelines considering many host countries have tight deadlines for arranging payroll tax filings and tax payments.

Review:

Compensation data review plays an important and critical role considering the host calculations are based on accuracy of data. Expatriate tax must ensure data received is thoroughly checked to avoid any discrepancies. Each component of paystub and expense reimbursement report must be reviewed to understand the exact nature of expense. This would help provide correct information to tax services provider during calculations.

Distribution:

Many companies use compensation tool to transfer data to tax services provider. However, it may not always be feasible to transfer data using a tool due to complexities such as data format, language, cost for tool set-up, etc. In such an event encrypted data sharing using workbooks is the best possible option.

Creating a standard template helps tax services provider understand and interpret the data correctly. The compensation workbook should ideally capture details in a single workbook to avoid multiple data sharing.

Standard compensation workbook template:

Individual Sheets
Pay stub description – earnings & deductions
Pay stub details – month wise, head wise
Expense reimbursement
Stock options (vested/exercised) – during assignment
Overseas Medical – health insurance
Employer Benefits – home & host country

Shadow Payroll

Shadow payroll is a payroll that doesn't physically pay the employee; rather it's a mechanism that allows the employer to meet their local payroll tax payments and reporting obligations by replicating or "shadowing" the home payroll compensation reporting. Shadow payroll is a method of calculating the appropriate tax and social security liabilities (in the host location) to be submitted to the host country authorities – while the employee continues to be paid from the home country payroll.

Essentially, the business entity or the payroll provider in the host country is required to "shadow" report all the payments and benefits that are paid in the home country. This also includes any other payments paid directly in the host country.

It is important to ensure that the home country payroll amounts are translated into host currency. In addition, local tax rules and reliefs should be applied, and, if necessary, calculate the tax gross up, especially if the employee is guaranteed a net pay.

Shadow payroll may sound simple, but it has its own share of challenges depending on; the home and host locations of the employee, employment status, and where costs are charged during assignment. It can be a complex process, which requires detailed knowledge and expertise making it crucial that companies are aware of any shadow payroll requirements when employees travel overseas – whether on a short or long-term basis.

Employees on International short-term or long-term assignments usually remain on home payroll and their stay in the host location may span 1-3 years. Many continue to remain on home social security and benefits where possible, having additional allowances and taxable costs associated with their assignment.

The assignment cost plus any gross ups of tax and host social security (if any) will need to be reported via the host payroll. Shadow payroll in these circumstances is usually a necessity and companies need to be certain that the host payroll receives the correct taxable income to ensure accurate and timely reporting.

If the employees do have a payroll requirement in the host location (i.e., not exempt through a tax treaty provision), the need to accurately calculate the correct payroll in the host location is even more important. In such circumstances, shadow payroll is again a necessity to manage any tax protection policies in place.

Tax Equalisation Settlements (TEQ)

Many companies take care of the incremental tax payments in Home and/or Host country arising due to international assignments. These can result in excess tax payments that are refundable since some countries follow the practice of taxing the global income regardless of whether any tax is paid also in the other country.

Due to complexities, expatriate tax usually seeks tax services provider assistance in filing tax returns in order to obtain appropriate tax credits / refund on the part of the tax borne under tax equalisation.

As part of the tax preparation and filing process tax services provider along with tax returns arrange to prepare a Tax Equalisation document that quantifies and communicates to employee the under or over funding of his/her hypothetical tax settlement.

TEQ should cover the following:

- Employee signature whereby he/she indicates agreement with the TEQ details presented by tax services provider

- If refund due from the tax authorities (Home/Host country), the employee agrees to settle the outstanding TEQ amount within 30 days of receiving the refund

Employees are required to fund 100% of the hypothetical tax obligation, regardless of their actual worldwide tax liability.

Manage Services of Tax Services Provider

Expatriate Tax role is to help prepare for the upcoming issues related to tax matters, often through assistance from in-house or external experts. It is important to monitor delivery of these services and assess employee satisfaction with them.

Expatriate Tax should be hands-on with managing global coordination. Due to the nature of assignment employees' work in different countries and in many cases companies may need to deal with multiple tax services providers.

Expatriate Tax should ensure periodic reports are shared by the services provider that captures real time status at country and employee level on Tax Briefing, Tax and Social Security ID registrations, Payroll filings, Tax return filings and so on.

On-going communication with both the expatriate and the provider – before, during, and after the assignment – will help ensure that the process is going as smoothly as possible.

CHAPTER 7

PERMANENT

ESTABLISHMENT

EXPOSURE

Global business expansions have put mobile employees on the rise. Tax authorities are eager to apply local corporate tax laws to companies operating within their borders. That's where the concept of Permanent Establishment (PE) comes into play. Tax authorities use permanent establishment as a tool to levy local taxes. This term is sometimes defined under a bilateral Income Tax Treaty between the host country and the country the business originates in.

Governments aim to apply their corporate tax laws to foreign companies operating within their country, so it's important for companies undertaking business activities in a foreign country to fully understand the risk of permanent establishment and learn how to mitigate it.

Companies with mobile employees doing business abroad must review where they stand and take permanent establishment risk seriously; else they may wake up one day with a big surprise of potential tax liability. It's thus important for companies operating in foreign countries to be aware of and understand the permanent establishment risk. Companies with mobile employees operating overseas must review its tax exposure, so it can accurately gauge its tax obligations and stay in compliance within a country.

What is Permanent Establishment?

Foreign country authorities want to know at what level a company is operating, so they can accurately assess income levels that may fall within the range of its corporate tax laws. This tax concept is known as permanent establishment. This scenario is what global tax consultants call "permanent establishment risk."

The risk of permanent establishment is that local tax authorities may deem a company operating within its jurisdiction a fixed place of business. If the tax authorities determine a company to be a fixed place of business, any revenue earned inside that country qualifies to be taxed accordingly based on local tax statutes and the amount of time the company is active as a permanent establishment.

What conditions/situations can lead to Permanent Establishment?

There are a number of activities companies might carry out which place them at an increased risk of being deemed as a permanent establishment. These may include but not limited to:

- Signing contracts with in-country businesses and profiting from those contracts
- Receiving payments from clients/customers operating within the same country and withholding taxes as a result
- Running business from a specific and set location on a regular or continuous basis
- Having access to a facility that isn't used exclusively for business but still remains in command of the business
- Using a mailing address in a foreign country for your company's location or bank account
- Making visits to a foreign country to provide maintenance on their product offerings, such as technical assistance or training
- Having employees visit the same site to carry out work on behalf of the company when they visit a country

- Sending employees to a foreign country to close a deal or work on behalf of the company in ways that generate revenue
- Having employees perform activity in a host country that directly generates revenue
- Withholding employee income and social security taxes

<u>What are the risks if a Permanent Establishment is not governed properly?</u>

Companies can face a number of threats and consequences. These may include but not limited to:

- Impairment to a business' reputation
- Impending regulatory issues
- Intensified audits from tax authorities
- Corporate tax liabilities
- Employer reporting requirements, including payroll and social security
- Immigration matters for employees
- Possible unanticipated tax cost if appropriate VAT registrations have not been made
- Penalties and interest charges

How to safeguard your organization from Permanent Establishment risk?

To steer your company through the intricacy of foreign country tax compliance and better defend it from permanent establishment risk, it is advisable to consider the following actions:

Work with a local tax specialist

Getting good tax advice from a local tax consultant lets you identify where your company stands, and how you can act accordingly. A reliable corporate tax advisor can support in reviewing any service contracts with employees and local business partners, provide guidance on local tax liabilities, and generally protect your company from any major tax obligations linked to permanent establishment risk exposures.

Engage with a local company

When the cost of establishing an entity in a foreign country is too high, working with a local establishment may be the best option for reducing permanent establishment risk. The local employer would be responsible for remitting all employer and employee taxes in compliance with local tax laws to avoid co-employment issues.

Establish a local business entity

To stay fully compliant with local tax authorities, a company can create a foreign subsidiary in its country of operation. A foreign subsidiary can operate independently from its parent company and would be responsible for its own assets and liabilities. It will be deemed to be a separate legal entity for taxation taking permanent establishment risk out in totality. This is by and large most expensive and time-consuming activity.

CHAPTER 8

OUTBOUND

ASSIGNMENT

MODELS

Organizations have many options when selecting their global mobility policy, and knowing the different types of international assignments can help them decide on their strategy.

With a diverse global mobility portfolio, organizations can maximize their Return on Investment by ensuring they choose the most appropriate and cost-effective assignment, whether concerning the duration of the assignment, location or its overall strategic goal.

Companies follow different types of assignment models as listed below:

- Short Term
- Long Term
- International Commuter
- Extended Business Travel
- Secondment
- Localization
- Permanent Transfer

Short term

A short-term assignment (STA) is an international assignment that usually lasts between 1 month and 12 months. This model allows organisations to transfer resources, knowledge and skills cost effectively.

While short term assignments sound simple, however they can pose some serious challenges for both the employer and employee. International short-term assignments can pose tax and immigration issues if companies do not comply with the laws and regulations in each country.

Long term

A long-term assignment (LTA) is an international assignment that usually lasts between 12 months and 36 months. Expatriates on long term assignments receive support including relocation benefits, housing allowances and annual home leave.

Global Mobility has moved from the traditional long term assignment programs that would cater to one policy for all expatriates. Companies are now altering their programs which provide different set of benefits based on assignment duration and job level. Benefits include tax counselling, immigration assistance, temporary living, education assistance, travel for self and dependant family members/partner to/from the host location, and home leave.

International Commuter

This is an alternative to international assignment; wherein an employee lives a few days of the week in the host country and frequently returns to home country.

International commuters are not defined by a specific type or length of the assignment. Employee tends to return home regularly over weekends or an entire week every month. In some cases, the employee travels between countries without a fixed schedule that are not controlled, termed as "frequent flier". Mobility must capture such travellers and track the number of days spent in the host country.

Extended Business Travel

Extended Business Travel (EBT) is a term for frequent business travellers who travel for business to different countries regularly for an extended period. Extended Business Travel is a mode to respond to client demands in other regions of the world. Mobility needs to pay attention to the duration of the stay.

Extended Business Travel has its own challenges. Tracking time spent at host country may be tougher because the rules around extended business travel are looser. When extended business travel exceeds 183 days, the agreement might trigger tax obligations in host countries. In a few countries based on local tax laws it may trigger tax obligations without crossing the threshold of 183 days.

Secondment

A secondment is an arrangement where a company temporarily assigns an employee to a new country and position. The new position may be within the organization or client or supplier. Under secondment, the home company usually retains the employee and pays their salary. Employees known as secondees, work on a project during their secondment period and return to their home country once they complete their responsibilities. During the secondment period the secondee works under the control of host organization.

A secondee who works for a different company keeps obligations to its original employer. A secondment agreement assigns the employees responsibilities that relate to the third-party organization. These responsibilities often dictate the employee's day-to-day duties and require them to adhere to the organization's policies.

Some secondments may allow the third-party organization to temporarily employ the secondee. In this situation, the third-party organization would be responsible for payment of salary and do a cross-charge. The contract must capture the terms and conditions of the secondment agreement.

Localization

Most international long-term assignments are between 12 months and 36 months. If the need for an employee exceeds 36 months, then the employee should be offered a local contract in the host country.

There are generally two scenarios of localization:

❖ Business-driven:

Most companies aim to localize an employee when they know an assignment is exceeding beyond 36 months. These are business-driven localizations and in this scenario, companies run a net-to-net calculation and use flexible guidelines for how to execute the compensation transition.

❖ Employee-initiated:

It's also worth mentioning employee-initiated localizations because they are often managed differently than business-driven ones. These are cases where the employee on assignment requests to stay in-country and move to local terms and conditions. When evaluating a request, companies consider different aspects, such as career potential in that location, criticality of the talent, work authorization limits, cost to the organization. There are often costs involved just to do the assessment – a net-to-net comparison, securing immigration and tax advice, etc. As a result, these localizations typically include only compliance support.

Permanent Transfer

Another commonly used relocation category is "Permanent Transfer". Permanent transfer is a one-way relocation of an employee to a Host country for an indefinite period. In a typical scenario, the individual will become an employee of the Host country entity, with Host country payroll and local benefits.

A transferee receives pay package as per local host country norms. Post permanent transfer employee is not tax equalized and many companies do not provide any tax compliance assistance. In a few circumstances based on seniority companies provide tax compliance only in the year of transfer. Permanent transfers are considered in scenarios where specific skills are required but not available in the Host location.

Post permanent transfer to local payroll, administrative costs are reduced as the Host country entity would handle only payroll reporting or withholding obligations. The risk of creating a permanent establishment presence for the home country entity is reduced as the individual would have severed employment ties with Home country entity.

A transferred employee receives compensation in Host country currency, and Host country benefits may differ from home country benefits. Post permanent transfer transferees are usually not eligible to contribute to home country retirement/benefit plans or contribute to home country social security, which may be a significant disadvantage for those that are at senior level or those approaching retirement.

CHAPTER 9

ON

ASSIGNMENT

(TO DO)

Income Tax & Social Security ID registration

More and more employees are being sent on international assignments by their companies. Many countries are imposing stricter regulations for foreign professionals and have now begun examining more closely even those foreign employees on short-term assignments to ensure they receive their share in taxes and social security contributions. In this respect, there is an increasing exchange of data between the immigration and tax authorities.

This now requires home companies to implement systems to monitor their employees' travel to host countries; otherwise they are liable to tax withholding payments or other penalties. Obligations under residency and work permit legislation are being reviewed thoroughly in the case of short-term and long-term assignments.

Tax and social security payments in host country require issuance of Unique Tax ID. Every individual on international assignment in order to comply with local tax regulations needs to apply for tax registration ID within a stipulated timeline on landing physically in host country.

A Taxpayer Identification Number (TIN) is a unique combination of numbers assigned by a country's tax authority to a person (individual or entity) and used to identify that person for the purposes of administering the country's tax laws. This Tax Identification Number should be included while making tax payments to ensure payments are allocated properly to individuals tax account.

For individuals, such functional equivalents may include a social security, health insurance number, personal identification/service code/number, or a resident registration number.

It is important for companies to gather country specific requirements before employee initiates international assignment as many non-English speaking countries may require documents to be attested by home country embassy (passport, birth certificate – self and dependant family members, marriage certificate, etc.)

In a few countries Tax and Social Security ID applications can be initiated online or may require physical visit to regulatory office in-person. In case employee has accompanying family members, separate application for Tax and Social Security may also be required.

Many countries permit Tax and Social Security ID applications through local tax services provider on employee behalf by gathering Power of Attorney (PoA).

Tax Return Filing

Post Tax year end (CY/FY) as per host country deadlines tax returns filing need to be initiated. Due to tax residency impact and other complexities many countries appoint local tax services provider to assist tax preparations. Returns must be filed electronically or via hard copy before due dates as per local tax regulations to avoid any late filing penalty.

Tax payments

Many countries follow Pay As You Earn (PAYE) concept, whereby either the employee or the employer needs to arrange tax payments to local authorities on monthly basis. Under this process tax and social security needs to be paid within specific timeline to avoid any penalty/interest.

Post Tax Year-end individual tax returns are file online or manually as per local host country regulation through tax services provider.

In a few countries taxes are computed by the tax services provider based on compensation data shared. A few countries require returns filing in tax portal wherein based on Income data shared the tax authorities assess the income and issue tax assessment order. Based on individual assessments by tax authorities, taxes are payable before due dates.

Many host countries allow employer to arrange tax payments on employee behalf from outside the host country via electronic transfer. The employer can arrange the tax payments ensuring correct individual Tax ID are allocated while arranging tax payments. In a few countries tax payments need to be arranged locally through the employee by physically visiting approved banks or at tax office.

It is important for companies or employees to gather tax payment receipts or confirmation from tax authorities /bankers of payment in the event of any future scrutiny notices.

Tax Residency Certificate

A Tax Residency Certificate (TRC) is a certificate issued by the home/host country revenue authorities to Tax residents who receive their income from countries with whom host country has an agreement for the avoidance of double taxation, known as the Double Taxation Avoidance Agreement (DTAA).

A Tax Residency Certificate helps evade double taxation. It is a levy of tax on the same income by two or more nations. To claim income tax relief under the DTAA treaty, a Tax Residency Certificate is mandatory from the tax authority of resident country.

 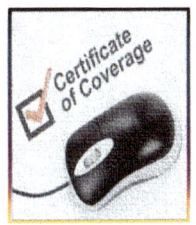

CHAPTER 10

IMPLICATIONS

OF SOCIAL

SECURITY

Social Security obligations can be one of the most significant contributions that employers will pay if they decide to send an employee on an international assignment. Social Security is also one of the most unnoticed aspects of the compensation package.

Social Security issues that alarm the employer's going on international assignment are as under:

- Will contributions to social security be required in the home country, host country, or both?
- Will the international assignment result in the employee losing any benefit entitlements?
- Will the employee be required to contribute towards social security in more than one country or must he/she contribute a larger amount overall had he/she stayed in the home country?
- Going beyond the contribution predicament, the employer will also have to administer how to deal with the situation should the employee stand to lose any benefit entitlements as a result of the international assignment?
- Will the employer need to consider whether to cover these additional costs on behalf of the employee?

European countries have the highest contribution rates, Asian and North American countries fall anywhere in the middle, whereas the lesser developing countries in Africa and Latin America are in the lower percentiles due to lack of advanced social security systems and policies.

While these situations are challenging, a number of bilateral totalization agreements (social security treaties between two countries) currently exist that help address concerns related to contributions thereby making the employer's task stress-free.

How Do Totalization Agreements Work?

Social security agreements vary in coverage, depending on the terms and conditions set down by the two contracting signatories. The principal purpose of such an agreement is to eliminate dual social security contributions, which occur when an employee from one country works in another country and is required to pay social security contributions to both countries on the same earnings.

Totalization agreements include an exception for international employees. Under this exception, a person who is temporarily assigned to work in another country remains covered only by the home country from which he / she has been sent. Both employee and employer must continue to pay contributions to the home social security system. Employees who are exempt from host social security contributions under a totalization agreement essentially need to document their exemption by obtaining a certificate of coverage (COC or A1) from the home country.

What Happens in Absence of Totalization Agreements?

Employees of countries in which no totalization agreement exists, are responsible for social security contributions to both their home and host country. In situations where no totalization agreement exists between the two countries, there may be extra costs for the employer.

These additional costs are:

- Mandatory employer-paid contributions to the host country social security program

- Reimbursement to the employee compensating for any extra expenditure incurred on social contributions as a result of the international assignment

The absence of an agreement is generally due to one of several possible reasons:

- Lack of rationality between the home country and host country social security systems

- Lack of international assignments sent to these countries

- Some countries only require permanent residents or nationals to contribute social security funds

- Lack of a social security system

What is A1 or Certificate of Coverage?

An A1 (formerly E-101) certificate is a document that states in which country the employee currently pays for social security contributions. Without an A1 certificate an employee cannot work in some countries. If an individual will be travelling for work in another EU member state, they will be required to have an A1 certificate before they travel.

Within EU policy, an individual can only be subject to one country's social security at a time. A1 certificates are typically considered when an individual is travelling to work and is therefore subject to social security contributions in their host country as well as their home country. By using an A1 certificate, (required in all EU and EEA countries plus Switzerland) the employee can prove current social security contributions in the home country and waive any social security contributions in the host country.

Globally Non-EU and non-EEA countries do not issue A1 statement but term the social security contribution exemption document as Certificate of Coverage. Certificate of Coverage (COC) or a detachment certificate is a document that must be obtained by an employee so as to avail the benefits under the applicable SSA. A Certificate of Coverage is issued in the employee's home country by the social security authority in accordance with the provisions of the relevant SSA.

Employees of non-European Economic Area (non-EEA) countries are responsible for contributions according to the specific treaty between their home and host country. These agreements vary by country, which generally permit the individuals to contribute to their home country social security program and not to the host country program, for an international assignment that ranges from one to five years, depending on the country.

- List of European Union (EU) countries:

    - Austria, Belgium, Bulgaria, Croatia, Republic of Cyprus, Czech Republic, Denmark, Estonia, Finland, France, Germany, Greece, Hungary, Ireland, Italy, Latvia, Lithuania, Luxembourg, Malta, Netherlands, Poland, Portugal, Romania, Slovakia, Slovenia, Spain and Sweden.

    - Iceland, Liechtenstein and Norway though not listed are permitted to be part of the EU member.

    - Switzerland is neither an EU or EEA member but permits Swiss nationals to live and work in the EU/EEA.

A1 Statement or Certificate of Coverage application process

Employers tend to be responsible for facilitating and applying for A1 or Certificate of Coverage certificates on behalf of their employees. In order to continue to be covered by the social security system in home country, employers must initiate application from the social security authority in the home country and inform the relevant host country's authorities ahead of anticipated travel. The application usually involves an online form and requires submitting the employee's personal information.

An A1 statement or Certificate of Coverage is a confirmation of which social security rules apply to employer or employee. The application form includes:

- country in which social security rules apply;
- country where the employee currently works;
- country where the employee will work;
- period for which the declaration is to be issued;
- grounds on which the social security legislation of the designated country applies

Validity of A1 Statement or Certificate of Coverage

A1 statement or Certificate of Coverage are usually valid for a period of 24 months, although the validity of each certificate can depend of the length of time the employee continues assignment in host country.

Benefits of A1 Statement or Certificate of Coverage

The main benefit is that employers and employees remain covered by their own country's social security system. By being covered under home country, employees will not need to pay social insurance contributions in the country they intend to temporarily work and live in.

CHAPTER 11

TAX CALENDAR –

RETURN FILING

DUE DATES

Countries globally follow Calendar year (CY) or Fiscal year (FY) concept for Tax return filings. Each country has different tax return filing deadline date that needs to be adhered.

Many countries strictly follow fixed return filing deadline date barring a few countries that allow extension for returns filing. It is thus very crucial to start the year end compliance process at least 3 – 4 months prior to the filing deadline date.

Companies must work closely with the employees and tax services provider to have the returns filing completion well before the filing due date to avoid payment of interest/penalty/both as the case may be.

Companies must use internal tools to initiate communication with the employees. Based on the assignment data (host country, start date, travel calendar) system generated mailers should be triggered to keep employees briefed of their tax filing obligations and due dates.

Companies must send periodic follow-up reminders (weekly or every other week) over email/mobile to employees covered under tax equalisation program to ensure return filing activities are on track.

The below table will give a broad overview of various host country tax return filing due dates and extensions possibility (if any).

List of Host countries following CY/FY - with filing deadline due dates

Tax Jurisdiction	Host country Tax Year (CY/FY)	Host country Tax Return Filing Deadline	Host country Tax Return Filing (Extension)
Australia	FY – ending June 30	31-Oct	Extension possible (generally 5 months post return filing deadline)
Belgium	CY	31-Oct	Extension possible (subject to tax authorities' approval)
Brazil	CY	29-Apr	No extension
Bulgaria	CY	30-Apr	No extension
Canada	CY	30-Apr	No extension
Denmark	CY	31-Jul	No extension
Egypt	CY	31-Jan	No extension
France	CY	20-May	No extension
Germany	CY	28-Feb	No extension
Hong Kong	FY– ending March 31	03-Jun	Extension possible (generally 2 months post return filing deadline)
India	FY– ending March 31	31-Jul	Extension possible (generally 2 months post return filing deadline)
Indonesia	CY	31-Mar	Extension possible (generally 2 months post return filing deadline)
Ireland	CY	31-Oct	Extension possible
Italy	CY	30-Sep	Extension possible (generally 2 months post return filing deadline)
Japan	CY	15-Mar	No extension
Malaysia	CY	30-Apr	No extension
Mauritius	FY– ending June 30	15-Oct	No extension
Netherlands	CY	01-May	Extension possible
New Zealand	FY– ending March 31	07-Jul	Extension possible (generally 9 months post return filing deadline)

Tax Jurisdiction	Host country Tax Year (CY/FY)	Host country Tax Return Filing Deadline	Host country Tax Return Filing (Extension)
Nigeria	CY	31-Mar	No extension
Philippines	CY	16-Apr	No extension
Poland	CY	30-Apr	No extension
Portugal	CY	30-Jun	No extension
Romania	CY	25-May	No extension
Singapore	CY	15-Apr	Extension possible (generally 3 months subject to tax authorities' approval)
South Africa	FY– ending February 28	24-Oct	Extension possible (generally 3 months post return filing deadline)
Taiwan	CY	31-May	No extension
Thailand	CY	31-Mar	No extension
United Kingdom	FY– ending April 5	31-Jan	No extension
United States of America	CY	15-Apr	Extension possible (generally 6 months post return filing deadline)
Vietnam	CY	30-Mar	No extension

CHAPTER 12

REPATRIATION /

END OF

ASSIGNMENT

Repatriation is a process of returning back from an international assignment to the home country after completing the assignment. Repatriation is the last step in the assignment life cycle and it involves re-entry of employee back to the home country.

There are many reasons an employee might need or want to be repatriated, such as:

- ❖ Natural end of the assignment
- ❖ Early end of the assignment because of project completion

Repatriation is a complicated process because there are a lot of parties involved. It would be ideal if a one-stop shop could help you through the repatriation process, but alas, that is not the case.

From immigration and expatriate tax point of view repatriation/end of assignment involves key to-dos:

- ❖ Cancellation of Resident Permit/Card/Work Permit
- ❖ Intimation of assignment completion to local municipal authorities and Immigration (Airport)
- ❖ Exit briefings with tax services provider
- ❖ De-registration of Tax & Social Security ID
- ❖ Filing – Exit Tax Return
- ❖ Payment of taxes (if any) – post exit return filing
- ❖ Procuring - Tax Clearance Certificate
- ❖ Cancellation of Certificate of Coverage / A1

Determination of RESIDENTIAL STATUS under Income Tax Act, 1961

CHAPTER 13

RESIDENTIAL

STATUS

IN INDIA

Residency impact

Residential status needs to be determined for every Fiscal year based on the individual's physical presence (regardless of the purpose of stay) in the respective Fiscal year. For calculating the number of days present during the relevant Fiscal year, the day of arrival into India and the day of departure from India should be considered as day present in India.

An individual would qualify as a Resident if either of the following two basic conditions is satisfied:

- He/ She stays in India for 182 days or more during the relevant Tax year/Fiscal year ('FY')

  (or)

- He/ She stays in India for 60* days or more during the relevant Fiscal year and 365 days or more in the four Fiscal year's immediately preceding the relevant Fiscal year

If both the aforesaid conditions are not fulfilled, the individual would be treated as Non-Resident in India during the relevant Fiscal year:

*The 60 days threshold shall be replaced by 182 days in case of the following:

- An Indian citizen leaving India for the purpose of employment outside India in the Fiscal year;

  (or)

- An Indian citizen or a person of Indian origin (PIO) comes on a visit to India in the relevant Fiscal year. However, as per the Finance Act, 2020, 60 days shall be replaced by 120 days in case of an Indian citizen or a

PIO having a total income, other than income from foreign sources, exceeding INR1,500,000(18,500 USD) during the relevant Fiscal year

As per the Finance Act, 2020, an individual would also be treated as a NOR if an Indian citizen or a PIO visiting India and having total income, other than income from foreign sources, exceeding INR1,500,000(18,500 USD) during the relevant Fiscal year stays for 120 days or more but less than 182 days in India during the relevant Fiscal year.

Simple flow chart – Residency in India

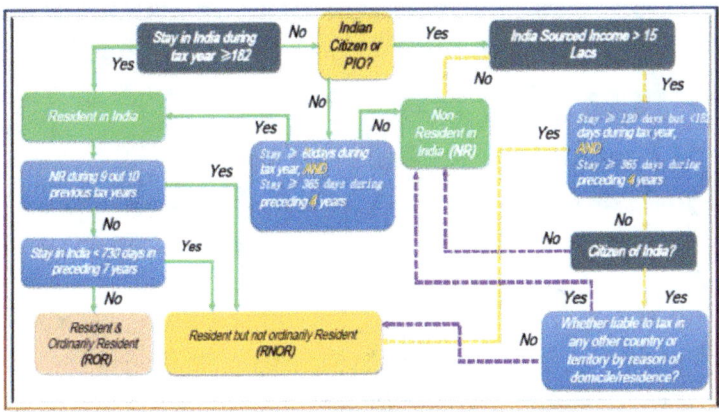

Double Taxation Avoidance Agreement (DTAA)

In case resident of one country (home/residence country) derives income from another country (host/source country) there arises a possibility of double taxation' of the same income in the source country and subsequently in the residence country. DTAA eliminates such double taxation of the same income.

Section 90 provides that where the provisions of the DTAA entered into by India with another country are more beneficial to any employee, the employee would be governed by such beneficial provisions of the DTAA subject to Tax Residency Certificate (TRC) being furnished by the employee.

Hence, in the case of an expatriate, the provisions of the DTAA need to be examined for the purpose of ascertaining the tax liability.

An expatriate being ROR of India, earning income in other country may be liable to tax in such country under the 'source' rule. However, he may also be liable to tax in respect of the same income in India as per the 'residence rule'. This scenario can lead to double taxation of the said income.

DTAA provide for specific provisions for elimination of such double taxation Article on elimination of double taxation/relief from double taxation of the DTAA provides that, the tax paid in source country shall be available as a credit in India However, to the extent of tax levied by India on such income.

Foreign Tax Credit (FTC)

An individual (qualifying as tax resident of India) must file Form No.67 before filing return of income to claim Foreign Tax Credit in his/her return of income.

Deemed Resident

An Indian citizen having a total income, other than income from foreign sources, exceeding INR1,500,000 (18,500 USD) during the relevant Fiscal year, will be deemed to be a resident in India, if he/ she is not liable to tax in any other country by reason of domicile, residence, or any other criteria of similar nature.

Being a Resident individual in India, it is important to determine whether an individual would be a ROR or NOR under the Act. An individual is treated as ROR if both the following additional conditions are satisfied:

- S/He qualifies as a Resident in India in two out of the ten Fiscal years' immediately preceding the relevant Fiscal year

    - **(and)**

- S/He stays in India for 730 days or more in the seven Fiscal years' immediately preceding the relevant Fiscal year

If both/ either of the aforesaid two conditions are not fulfilled, the individual would be treated as NOR in India during the relevant Fiscal year.

Taxability based on Residential Status:

Timing of the assignment – commencement, completion and total tenure– defines Residential Status

- ROR is taxable on the **global income**. In other words, ROR is taxable in India in respect of the following:
  - Income received in India;
  - Income accruing or arising in India or deemed to accrue or arise in India;
  - Income accruing or arising outside India or deemed to accrue or arise outside India

- NR/ NOR is taxable on income sourced or received in India. In other words, NR/ NOR is taxable in India in respect of the following:
  - Income directly received in India;
  - Income accruing or arising in India or deemed to accrue or arise in India

In addition to the above points, NOR is also taxable on the income from business or profession that is controlled wholly or partly in India.

Residential Status of an Individual	Scope of Taxable Income in India
ROR	Global income
NOR	Income sourced or directly received in India
NR	Income sourced or directly received in India

Analysis of Residential Status:

Brief on Residential Status

The taxability in India would depend on the residential status, which in turn, would depend on the individual's physical presence in India. The residential status of an individual can be classified into two categories as follows:

- Resident (ROR)
- Non-Resident (NR)

Simple understanding of ROR and NR

- Resident in India (ROR)
    - Spends > 182 days in India – specific tax year (start of assignment)

    OR

    - Spends ≥ 59 days in India – specific tax year (end of assignment)
- Non-Resident in India (NR)
    - Spends < 182 days in India – specific tax year (start of assignment)

    OR

    - Spends ≤ 59 days in India – specific tax year (end of assignment)

Why do refunds arise in India Tax Returns?

Unlike most countries, India does not provide the option at returns filing stage wherein Tax authorities allow employee declaration to have tax refund credits into employer account in the event taxes are paid by employer on employee behalf.

Refunds in India can only be credited to employee bank account registered in tax portal. Based on the tax residency in India refund/tax credits are available.

There are usually two main categories/reasons for tax refunds arising at returns filing stage.

Resident and Ordinary Resident (ROR)

- **Double Tax Avoidance Agreement (DTAA)**
  - Tax treaty signed between India and another country
  - Taxpayers can avoid paying double taxes on same income
  - Provide relief to employees in the form of refund of the tax paid twice

Non-Resident (NR)

- **Dependent Personal Service (DPS)**
  - Tax exempt in India if Resident of host country
  - Applicable to employees performing their services in a country other than the country of their residence

CHAPTER 14

COMPLIANCE

REQUIREMENTS

IN INDIA

Outbound Expatriates

In case of a person domiciled in India, leaving India the relevant information needs to be furnished to the Indian tax authorities in Form No.30C which is a self-declaration by the outbound expatriate that includes his/her details such as PAN, Passport details, purpose of visit outside India and estimated period of stay outside India, etc.

Based on the information submitted in Form No. 30C, the Income Tax Authority, if considers it necessary may require a person who is domiciled in India and leaving India to obtain Tax Clearance Certificate in Form No.33 by making an application in Form No.31.

Inbound Expatriates

Before Arrival:

Foreign nationals arriving in India must hold valid visa or travel authorization.

Foreign nationals can secure below illustrative list of visas to enter India depending upon their purpose to visit India:

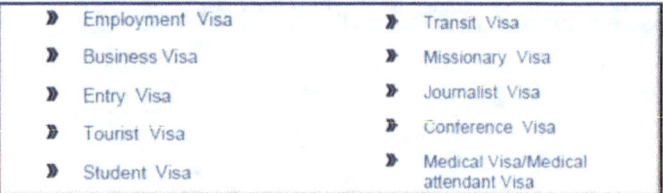

Foreign nationals have to obtain Employment/Business Visa for taking up employment in India – OCI Card holders can get employed without employment visa.

Employment Visa – key considerations

For highly skilled/qualified foreign nationals seeking employment in India

- Not granted for routine/ordinary jobs where large number of Indian nationals are available
- Granted in annual salary>INR1,625,000 (20,000 USD), including allowances and perquisites
- Granted for a period of 5 years including renewals

Business Visa– key considerations

- Granted for bonafide business reasons only for specified activities including;
  - Establishing a business venture or exploring opportunities to set up business
  - Attending technical meetings, discussions, board meetings, general meetings to provide business support service
  - Participating in an exhibition or trade fair
  - Foreign trainees attending in-house training
  - Foreign nationals engaged in commercial sports events in India
  - Foreign experts and specialists on a short duration visit in connection with an on-going project with the objective of monitoring the progress of the work, conducting meetings with Indian customers and/or to provide technical guidance

- Duration shall normally be 6 months, 1 year, 5 years subject to agreement between two governments, allowing single or multiple entries. Period of each visit can be restricted to a maximum of 6 months.

After Arrival:

Foreigners' Registration

Foreign nationals visiting India are generally required to get themselves registered with concerned Foreigner's Registration Office ('FRRO/FRO') where the validity of visa exceeds 180 days or within the stipulated time period as endorsed on visa (if any). Generally foreign nationals are required to obtain registration within 14 days of arrival in India. Penalty is applicable if there is a delay in registration.

Provisions related to Visa extension

Generally, long term visas such as Employment, Business, Entry(X), etc., are extendable on year-to-year basis.

Surrender of Residential Permit

While finally exiting India, post completion of Indian assignment, the foreign nationals are required to surrender residential permit to the concerned FRRO/FRO or the immigration officer at the Immigration check point.

Foreign nationals need to inform the FRO in case change in accommodation and obtain certificate of change of address.

Table – Inbound and Outbound requirements

In-bound Expatriates	Out-bound Expatriates
Registration of Foreign National with Foreigners Regional Registration Officer (FRRO)	-
Opening of Bank Account in India	-
Permanent Account Number (PAN)	Permanent Account Number (PAN)
Return of Income	Return of Income
Form 67 along with Return of Income if claiming Foreign Tax Credit (FTC) in Return of Income in India	Form 67 along with Return of Income if claiming Foreign Tax Credit (FTC) in Return of Income in India
-	Certificate of Coverage to claim exemption from the host country's social security
Undertaking to be furnished by a person not domiciled in India at the time of his departure from India in Form No. 30A	Information to be furnished by a person domiciled in India at the time of his departure from India in Form No. 30C
Income Tax Authority shall on receipt of such undertaking in Form No. 30A, immediately give to such person a no objection certificate (Tax Clearance Certificate) for leaving India in Form No. 30B	Income Tax Authority, if considers it necessary, may require such person to obtain Tax Clearance Certificate in Form No. 33 by making an application in Form No. 31
Surrender of Residential Permit post completion of Indian assignment to the concerned FRRO/FRO	-

CHAPTER 15

SOCIAL SECURITY

OBLIGATION

IN INDIA

Employer and Employee are liable to contribute to Employees' Provident Fund (EPF) under Indian law subject to relief, if any, under a Social Security Agreement. Outbound expatriate employees contributing to foreign social security scheme pursuant to their posting to a foreign country in absence Social Security Agreement between India and such foreign country can still contribute to Provident Fund in India if they continue to be employees of Indian employer during the period of their assignment and continues to receive salary in India.

Social Security in India is predominantly governed by the Employees' Provident Funds and Miscellaneous Provisions Act, 1952 (the EPF Act). Employers employing 20 or more employees are governed under the EPF Act.

EPF Act contains the following three principal schemes:

- Employees Provident Funds Scheme, 1952 (EPF Scheme)
- Employees' Pension Scheme, 1995(Pension Scheme)
- Employees Deposit Linked Insurance Scheme, 1976(EDLI scheme)

The applicability of the existing Provident Fund and Pension Schemes was extended to "International Workers" (IW) with effect from November 1, 2008. International Worker is defined as: "A foreign national working for an establishment in India to which the EPF Act applies". It also includes: "An Indian employee who divides his career between India and another country and that country should be one with which India has a social security agreement."

Exclusion to International Worker:

A foreign national from country with which India has entered into a Social Security Agreement ('SSA') is excluded from Indian social security contribution. However, in order to avail the exemption, the employer needs to obtain certificate of coverage (COC) from the home country.

Employees Provident Fund Organisation (EPFO) has clarified Indian expatriates who qualify as International Workers while on employment abroad would become domestic employees once they come back to India.

Both the employer and employee are required to contribute 12% of "monthly pay" under the EPF regulations. The employer also has to make 0.5% contribution (capped at a monthly salary of INR15,000) towards EDLI scheme which is an insurance scheme under the EPF Act.

For International Workers, the wage ceiling of INR15,000 is not applicable and contributions are required to be made on full monthly pay. Pay means Basic Salary, Dearness allowance (including cash value of food concession) and Retention allowance, etc.

Table – International Workers EPF/EPS contribution

Particulars	IW who has joined before 01-09-2014 or who is an existing member of PF	IW who has joined and become member of PF for the 1st time on or after 01-09-2014 and having monthly pay which exceeds the statutory limit of Rs. 15,000
Employee's Contribution to PF Scheme	12% of Monthly Pay	12% of Monthly Pay
Employer's contribution to PF Scheme	3.67% of Monthly Pay	12% of Monthly Pay
Employer's contribution to Pension Scheme	8.33% of Monthly Pay	-
Total Contribution	24% of Monthly Pay	24% of Monthly Pay

Social Security Agreements (SSA)

India has currently signed Social Security Agreement's with 20 countries of which, SSA's with 19 countries are effective and in force. Out of total 19 operative Social Security Agreement's, 14 are with European country and other 5 are with Australia, Canada, Japan, Quebec and Republic of Korea.

Social Security Agreement (SSA) with INDIA (in force)		
Sr. No.	Country	Date in Force
1	Austria	01 July 2015
2	Australia	01 January 2016
3	Belgium	01 September 2009
4	Canada	01 August 2015
5	Czech Republic	01 September 2014
6	Denmark	01 May 2011
7	Finland	01 August 2014
8	France	01 July 2011
9	Germany	01 October 2009
10	Hungary	01 April 2013
11	Japan	16 November 2012
12	Luxembourg	01 June 2011
13	Netherlands	01 December 2011
14	Norway	01 January 2015
15	Portugal	04 March 2013
16	Quebec	26 November 2013
17	Republic of Korea	01 November 2011
18	Sweden	01 August 2014
19	Switzerland	29 January 2011

CHAPTER 16

EXCHANGE

CONTROL IN

INDIA

Bank Accounts:

Banks offer two types of accounts to Person Resident Outside India/Non-Resident Indians, based on whether funds available in the account are repatriable i.e. whether such funds can be transferred or repatriated abroad.

Different Types of Bank Accounts:

- Non-Resident (External) Rupee Account (NRE Account)
- Foreign Currency (Non-Resident) Account (FCNR Account)
- Non-Resident Ordinary Account (NRO Account)
- Resident Foreign Currency Account (RFC Account)

Remittance of Salary

A citizen of a foreign state resident in India or a citizen of India, employed by a foreign entity outside India and on deputation to India with the office/branch/subsidiary/joint venture/group company in India of such foreign entity or being an employee of an Indian entity may open, hold and maintain a foreign currency account with a bank outside India and receive/remit the whole salary payable to him/her for the services rendered, by credit to such account provided that income tax chargeable under the Income Tax Act is paid on the entire salary as accrued in India.

However, a foreign national not on deputation but in direct employment with an Indian company shall need to receive his salary in India and then remit the same (after payment of appropriate taxes) overseas.

Permissible investments

The permissible investments for different categories of individuals under the foreign exchange laws in India are tabulated as under:

Status of Individual	Investments	General / Special Permission
Non-Resident Indian Person of Indian Origin/ Overseas Citizen of India	Shares, convertible debentures, real estate (other than an agricultural land, plantation property or farm house etc.)	General Permission granted
Foreign National	Shares, convertible debentures	General Permission granted
	real estate (including an agricultural land, plantation property or farm house)	Not permitted

CHAPTER 17

BEST

PRACTICES

In order to exercise high degree of skill, diligence, prudence and foresight it is important for global mobility and expatriate tax professionals to comply with all guidelines, documents and codes of practice considering the complexities and risks of international assignment. Implementing a few methods from time to time would reasonably and ordinarily be expected to be used by a skilled professional.

Best Practices:

- ❖ Alignment with key stakeholders
- ❖ Create internal tool to derive host country tax cost
- ❖ Create accruals in company books (host country)

✦ Alignment with key stakeholders

Coordinating with internal stakeholders globally tends to be the biggest challenge in mobility. The global mobility function must engage with a broad spectrum of stakeholders. Mobility must play a key role in ensuring all stakeholders are aligned globally for safeguarding company interest and its mobile employees are compliant with necessary host obligations.

Global mobility needs to work hand-in-hand with Business, Payroll, Finance, Tax, Employment Legal, Human Resources and Immigration. Global mobility professionals need to be multi-lingual when it comes to managing diverse stakeholders. Global mobility must invest time for stakeholder engagement. Getting to know all stakeholders individually rather than categorizing them should take priority.

The compliance aspect of global mobility generally leads to a perception that mobility is hindering rather than helping its stakeholders to achieve their objectives. Hence global mobility function should maintain a regular and on-going dialogue with stakeholders. It is critical to understand the diverse needs of different stakeholder groups.

Global mobility professionals need to be regularly checking with stakeholders whether or not they are on track to achieve their objectives as by supporting them there is a much greater probability of succeeding.

♦ Create internal tool to derive host country tax cost

Companies should create an internal tool (simple workbook) that helps derive the likely tax and social security (payroll tax) liability in the host country. The liability calculation need not be 100% accurate, however it will certainly help analyse the likely tax impact. Worldwide personal tax summaries/guides are freely available on the internet that help provide most updated tax and social security progressive / flat rates that can be a good start for computing the host liability.

In most countries Income tax and Social security liabilities are calculated considering compensation/pay stub details and expense reimbursement in home & host country. The workbook should factor these costs while computing the liability on Calendar Year or Fiscal Year basis, as per host country tax year end. The internal calculations help review with actuals in the event of any huge tax variations as shared by tax services provider.

Steps – Payroll Tax computation

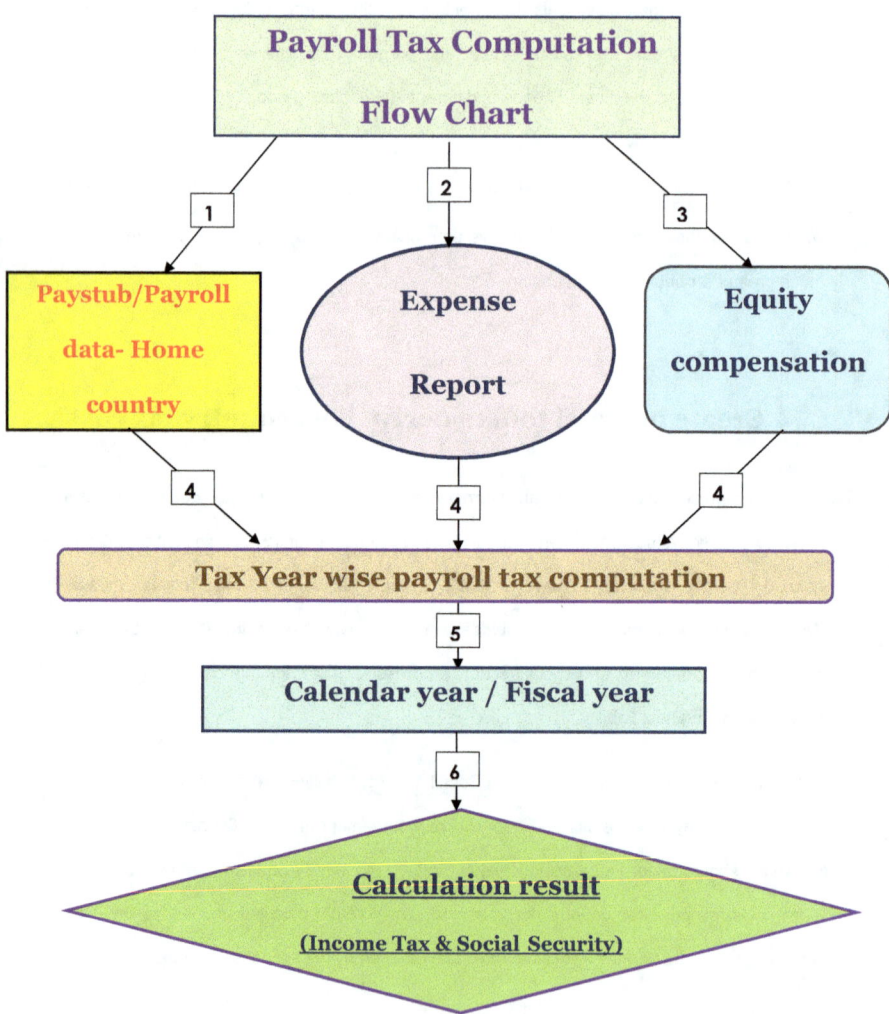

Payroll Tax Computation Flow Chart

1 → **Paystub/Payroll data- Home country**

2 → **Expense Report**

3 → **Equity compensation**

4 → **Tax Year wise payroll tax computation**

5 → **Calendar year / Fiscal year**

6 → **Calculation result** (Income Tax & Social Security)

✦ Create accruals in company books (host country)

Companies should diligently work towards creating accruals in company books on international assignment costs related to tax, social security, health insurance and professional fees.

✦ Income Tax and Social Security

Companies should build a process to book payroll tax accruals liability on a quarterly basis as this gives confident to the stake holders and internal/external auditors the company is serious about compliance.

✦ Professional fees (tax services provider)

Most companies who seek external tax services provider assistance create standard yearly Statement of Work (SOW) that captures various activities on host tax compliance and fees involved at country and individual level. It is thus important to create quarterly accruals that can help reconcile the actual fees post billing.

✦ Professional fees accruals should detail:

- ❖ Shadow payroll calculations
- ❖ Income and Social tax Id registrations
- ❖ Year-end tax returns preparation/filings
- ❖ Income and Social tax Id de-registrations
- ❖ Response to tax notices
- ❖ Tax Residency Certificate
- ❖ Out of scope services

Special Thanks/Acknowledgements:

This book is a compilation of my experiences and thanks to everyone who has been a part to them. Thanks to the many bosses I have had over the years and especially to my mentor and guide Nancy Dwan, Senior Director – Employee Assignments with Oracle Corporation in California, USA for her immense support and direction. Under her leadership I gained enormous exposure and learning on global mobility and expatriate tax, without which I would not be in a position that I am today to be able to put across an informative handbook from a global perspective. Thank you, Nancy.

I would like to thank Makarand Padalkar, Whole Time Director and Chief Financial Officer with Oracle Financial Services in Mumbai, India who inspired me to take the book idea to reality. It was his confidence and belief in me that my knowledge on mobility tax should be penned down in a book. Thank you, Makarand.

I would like to thank my friend and guide Rajiv Thadani, Principal, Global Mobility Services with KPMG LLP in California, USA who read every chapter, and his feedback on everything has been invaluable. Thank you, Rajiv, for living this journey with me.

I would like to thank Parizad Sirwalla, Partner and Head, Global Mobility Services, Tax – KPMG in India for her valuable feedback on the contents covered in the handbook. Thank you, Parizad.

I would like to thank Sundeep Agarwal, Partner, Global Mobility Services with Vialto Partners (formerly PwC), in Mumbai, India for his encouragement, support and valuable feedback on the contents covered in the handbook. Thank you, Sundeep.

Disclaimer:

The information contained herein should not be treated as an alternative to seeking guidance from tax experts. This book should be used as a ready reckoner to understand mobility tax from a global perspective.

The author will bear no liability for errors, omissions, or inadequacies in the information contained herein or for interpretations thereof.

If you need any consulting advice to setup, streamline, review your organizations mobility program feel free to connect at: paggy.tipnis@gmail.com